May aLL of God's chiLdren come
to know the babe of BethLehem.
—DWH

Dedicated to the Love of my Life, Addison.
And to my Loving family who've always believed in me.
—Aubrie

Text © 2018 Dona Wilding Haws
Illustrations © 2018 Aubrie Moyer

ISBN 13: 978-1-4621-2273-8

Published by CFI, an imprint of Cedar Fort, Inc.
2373 W. 700 S., Springville, UT 84663
Distributed by Cedar Fort, Inc., www.cedarfort.com

Library of Congress Control Number: 2018946716

Cover design and typesetting by Shawnda T. Craig
Cover design © 2018 Cedar Fort, Inc.
Edited by Kaitlin Barwick

Printed by Artin Printing Co.
82485
8-13-18

Printed in South Korea

10 9 8 7 6 5 4 3 2 1

Printed on acid-free paper

Are You the Babe of Bethlehem?

Written by **Dona Wilding Haws** · Illustrated by **Aubrie Moyer**

CFI · An imprint of Cedar Fort, Inc. · Springville, Utah

Have you seen
the babe of Bethlehem?

No, I am not the babe of Bethlehem. I am Zacharias.

Angel Gabriel came to me while I was serving in the temple. He stood to the right of the altar of incense. Angel Gabriel told me that my wife, Elisabeth, would have a baby boy, even though we are old.

Luke 1:5-19

Luke 1:57–64,
Matthew 3:13–17

Are you the babe of Bethlehem?

No, I am not the babe of Bethlehem.
I am Elisabeth, wife of Zacharias.

I am going to have a baby boy, and we will name him John. When he grows up, people will call him John the Baptist. John will baptize Jesus.

Luke 1:11–19, 26–35

Are you the babe of Bethlehem?

No, I am not the babe of Bethlehem. I am angel Gabriel.

First, I visited Zacharias in the temple in Jerusalem. Six months after I visited Zacharias, God sent me to visit Mary in Nazareth. God was very pleased with Mary. God sent me to tell Mary that she would become the mother of the true babe of Bethlehem.

Are you the babe
of Bethlehem?

No, my dear one, I am not
the babe of Bethlehem. I am Mary.

I am the mother of the precious babe
of Bethlehem. Angel Gabriel came to
me telling me that this would be so.
Angel Gabriel said, "Fear not, Mary:
for thou hast found favour with God.
And, behold, thou shalt conceive in
thy womb, and bring forth a son, and
shalt call his name Jesus."

Luke 1:26-38

Are you the babe of Bethlehem?

No, my boy, I am not the babe of Bethlehem. I am Joseph.

The angel of the Lord came to me in a dream to tell me about
the babe of Bethlehem. I will protect Mary and the sweet baby.
We will name him Jesus, just as the angel told me to do.

Matthew 1:20-21

Are you the babe of Bethlehem?

No, little one, I am not the babe of Bethlehem. I am the innkeeper.

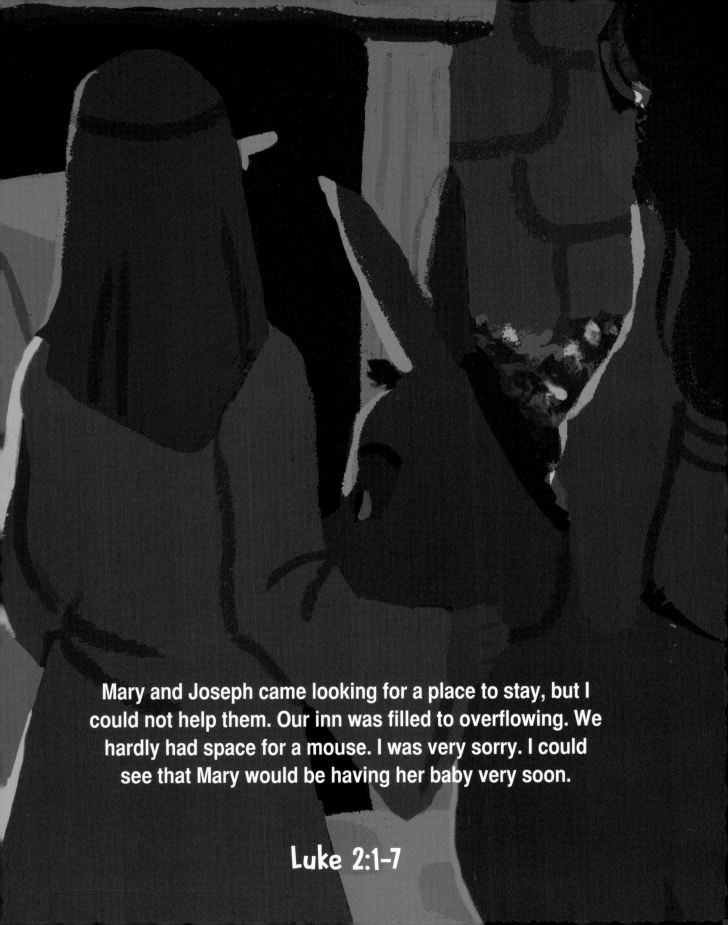

Mary and Joseph came looking for a place to stay, but I could not help them. Our inn was filled to overflowing. We hardly had space for a mouse. I was very sorry. I could see that Mary would be having her baby very soon.

Luke 2:1-7

Are you the babe of Bethlehem?

No, my little friend, I am not the babe of Bethlehem. I am an angel.

God sent me to tell the shepherds that the wonderful babe of Bethlehem was born. It was in the dark of night when I appeared to the shepherds. The glory of the Lord shone all around us. I said, "Fear not: for, behold, I bring you good tidings of great joy." That very day, Jesus Christ was born to be the Savior of the world.

Luke 2:8-12

Are you the babe of Bethlehem?

No, we are not the babe of Bethlehem. We are shepherds.

We were watching our sheep when the angel appeared and said we would "find the babe, wrapped in swaddling clothes, and lying in a manger." After the first angel, a multitude of heavenly hosts came, praising God and saying, "Glory to God in the highest, and on earth peace, good will toward men."

Luke 2:8-14

We rushed to Bethlehem to find the blessed baby.
And just as the angel said, baby Jesus was wrapped
in swaddling clothes and lying in a manger.
We worshipped the heaven-sent baby with humble
hearts. When we left, we told the wonderful news to
everyone we saw. We glorified and praised God for
all we had heard and seen.

Luke 2:15-16, 20

Are you the babe of Bethlehem?

No, we are not the babe of Bethlehem.
We live in Bethlehem.

The shepherds told everyone they saw about the blessed baby who would become the Savior of the world. It is amazing! Awesome! Wonderful!

Luke 2:11, 17-18

Are you the babe of Bethlehem?

No, I am not the babe of Bethlehem. I am King Herod.

I heard that wise men had come from the East, looking for a new king of the Jews. So I called my scribes and priests to find out where this child would be born. The ancient prophet wrote that He would be born in Bethlehem. I talked to the wise men secretly, telling them to go to Bethlehem and to come back and tell me when they found the child.

Matthew 2:1-8

We had seen His star, and we came searching for the newborn king of the Jews. We talked with King Herod, and he told us to go to Bethlehem. The star guided us. We rejoiced when we found the blessed babe of Bethlehem. We worshipped the holy child. We gave him our treasures—gold and frankincense and myrrh.

Are you
the babe of
Bethlehem?

Yes, my little one.

Luke 2:7-18,
Matthew 2:1-12

I was the babe born in the stable, wrapped in
swaddling clothes, and laid in a manger.

Angels came to the shepherds, and the shepherds came to the stable.
The shepherds told everyone they saw.

The wise men came from the east with gifts of gold, frankincense, and myrrh.

Are you really the babe of Bethlehem?
Have I found you at Last?

Matthew 3:16-17

Yes, my dear one. You have found me.

You have found the babe of Bethlehem—all grown up.
I am Jesus Christ, the son of God.
I am the babe of Bethlehem.